INSTAGRAN

INSTAGRAN

An Hachette UK Company
www.hachette.co.uk

Summersdale Publishers Ltd
Part of Octopus Publishing Group Limited
Carmelite House
50 Victoria Embankment
LONDON
EC4Y 0DZ
UK

www.summersdale.com

Printed and bound in Malta

ISBN: 978-1-78685-206-9

Substantial discounts on bulk quantities of Summersdale books are available to corporations, professional associations and other organisations. For details contact general enquiries by telephone: +44 (0) 1243 771107 or email: enquiries@summersdale.com.

This book is not endorsed by, promoted by or associated with Instagram™.

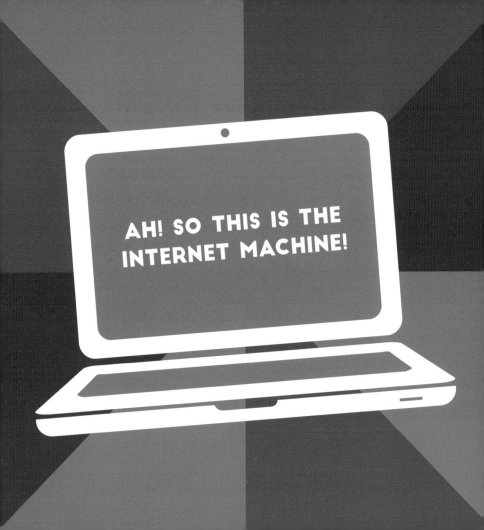

Single, and she's
only three miles away!

WHAT ON EARTH IS
KEVIN PUTTING ON
FACEBOOK NOW?!

Now type 'Jimmy is my least favourite grandchild'. That'll teach Joan to leave herself logged in...

It's not actually real money when you buy shoes online, is it?

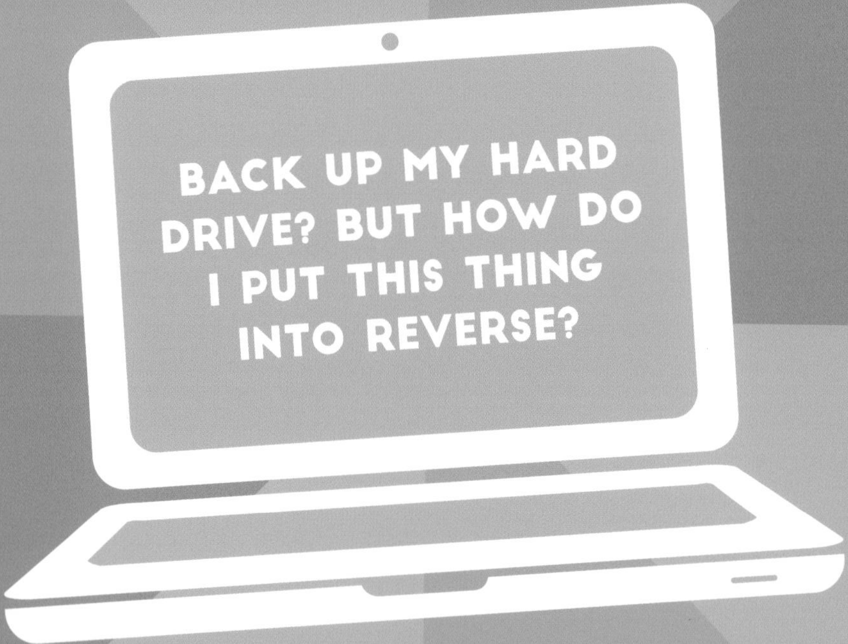
BACK UP MY HARD DRIVE? BUT HOW DO I PUT THIS THING INTO REVERSE?

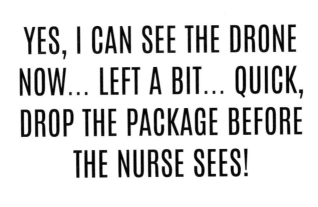

So... they've invented wireless defibrillators now?

But it says if I just fill
in my bank details I'll
win a free holiday to Bali!

I can't have a virus...
I had my flu vaccine
only last week!

Well, I guess I do like it 'wet, hot and wild', now that you ask...

MARGARET, I KNOW YOU ASKED ME TO WATCH THESE SHOES ON EBAY, BUT IT'S BEEN FIVE HOURS AND I'M STARTING TO GET A BIT TIRED...

There we go. I've
deleted Uncle Steve
off Facebook
for you.

It's a webcam, Grandad, and I can still only see the top of your head!

OH, YOU WANTED TO FIND SOME GRANDFATHER *CLOCKS*? LET'S TRY THAT SEARCH AGAIN...

MY GRANDSON SAID HE'S GOING TO GIVE ME A BLUE TOOTH. I NEED ALL THE TEETH I CAN GET NOWADAYS.

I've set our relationship status to 'Divorced'!

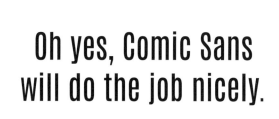

I think I'll use my iTunes credit on Jay-Z's new stuff.

There's Lorraine and
Bill's house, right there!
Let's call them and ask
them to step outside
and wave.

HI SON, WHAT CHANNEL
IS THE NETFLIX ON?

I don't know why the thing's frozen — it's lovely and warm out here.

Oh yes, the bunny-face filter really does make me look hot.

BUT WHY DO I NEED TO OPEN A NEW WINDOW? IT'S ALREADY FAR TOO COLD IN HERE.

SET YOUR PASSWORD AS 'INCORRECT', DEAR. THEN, WHEN YOU FORGET IT, THE COMPUTER TELLS YOU 'YOUR PASSWORD IS INCORRECT'.

Try again, love – I think I had my eyes closed that time --

Wait until they see
the memes I've got
in store...

NOW I'VE PUT MY GLASSES ON, CAN YOU SEE ME BETTER?

OK, I'M READY TO BECOME A YOUTUBE SENSATION. NOW, HOW DO I TURN THIS THING ON AGAIN?

Amazing –
I’m the millionth
visitor! This is our
lucky day!

Err, you're taking a picture of the ceiling, Maureen.

CAPTION THAT ONE
#SQUADGOALS, LINDA!

I think I could easily
be a video-logger too,
you know.

Darling, you need to take two pictures, so you can give one to me.

THIS SEASON
OF *AMERICAN
HORROR STORY* IS
SOMETHING ELSE.

THAT'S VERY NICE, DEAR,
BUT CAN WE GO BACK
TO LOOKING AT THE
FUNNY CATS?

So how do we take the photo when the button is so far away?

My email password's been hacked again? But I've already had to rename the cat twice.

So, petal, you're telling me that emails still get delivered on a Sunday, right?

CAN'T BELIEVE I'VE BEEN
PLAYING *MINECRAFT*
ALL NIGHT.

I'M STARTING TO THINK THERE NEVER WERE ANY HOT, YOUNG SINGLES IN MY AREA.

You see, back in my day we'd be in big trouble if we wrote on someone's wall!

I DON'T CARE IF IT WAS A SCAM — I'D LIKE THE MONEY I WAS PROMISED!

I can't believe these toenail clippers that I bought from the Amazon have next-day delivery!

Sending the invite out on Facebook now... This party is gonna be lit!

SO GLAD WE DON'T HAVE TO DO ANY OF THIS ONLINE DATING NONSENSE.

How do I tweet, when I'm not a bird?

If we stay perfectly still, Johnny will think Skype has frozen again.

WHAT DO YOU MEAN,
YOU CAN SEE THE
INSIDE OF MY EAR?

IMAGE CREDITS

Snapcat

The cats that love
to snap (and chat)

SNAPCAT

ISBN: 978 1 78685 195 6   **Hardback**   **£7.99**

Join the cats that snap and discover the candid stories of their daily lives. These cool kitties have a lot to say, and whether it's with a cheeky filter or a sassy caption, they say it with style. You'll see your fur-miliar friends through a whole new lens.

If you're interested in finding out more
about our books, find us on Facebook at
Summersdale Publishers and follow us on
Twitter at **@Summersdale**.

www.summersdale.com